VICISSITUDE OF

DESTINY

First Volume:

- △ Sexuality Diversity
- △ Disturbing Thoughts
- △ Bribe

By: East West Man

Translated by: Piter Seloon

Title: Vicissitude of Destiny (First Volume)

Author: East West Man

Translator: Piter Seloon

Publisher: Supreme Century, USA

ISBN: 978-1939123787

In the Name of the Creator

Introduction

With the growth of industry and the expansion of societies, some personal and social problems such as Sexuality diversity, abusive thoughts, bribery and …… have grown, too. Some of such a dilemma can affect people mental and physical health that If not corrected, it would simply lead to moral corruption, cause families to be disintegrated/collapsed and would have some irreparable harm. In this book, there are simple shapes and contexts for the treatment of such problems. Once, drawing the shapes and reading the sentences makes our busy mind pay attention to a simple relationship which has been as law in the minds of every human being since the moment of the birth; the relationship between God and the power of the mind to control the negative intelligent forces and the sins committed during their previous lives. As science, technology and industry progress, due to inaccurate information, and poorly religious teachings this relationship has been cut off or diminished more than ever. Its failure has been the cause of the weakness of a protective shield against entering negative intelligence into the shafts/bodies and causing the people in the community to be vulnerable.

Sexuality

Diversity

Omid heard the bell sound indicating a text has arrived; he looked at his cell phone. When he thought of his new girlfriend's body, he felt sweetness on the tip of his tongue. At sunset, when the office closed, he drove his car to the restaurant; his girlfriend was sitting at one of the tables in the restaurant wearing makeup and a fashionable dress.

Omid shook his girlfriend's hand and sat down on a seat.

- When did you arrive?

The girl frowned and replied, "Half an hour ago. Why are you late?"

- The plane landed a bit late. It was silent for a few moments.

The girl asked, "What is your job?"

Looking around Omid replied, "I own a commercial company."

The girl said, "Oh. Married?"

- Yeah. But I don't like my wife.

The girl ate a little tea, saying nothing. A few minutes later Omid's cell phone rang. His girlfriend was watching him. Omid picked up the phone. Sara was calling him on another line. She asked, "Where are you?"

Omid's face changed color. He swallowed his saliva with difficulty and said in a panic, "Something came up; I'll be late; eat your dinner!"

She had the rest of the tea while the glass was in her hand; laughed and said, "Was it your wife?"

-Yeah.

The girl said, "What's the panic for you now?"

Omid didn't say anything.

The girl continued, "So you love her!"

- I don't want to ruin my life.

The girl asked, "So why are you looking for a girlfriend?"

- Omid was bored, looking at the menu and said, "Never mind. What would you like to have?"

Eating the dinner was over. Omid gave her girlfriend a ride to her home and went towards his home. When he arrived, it was late at night; Sarah was sitting alone at the dining table. Three meals were sitting on the table. Glancing at him, Sarah put her hand under her chin and stared at the table; she knew since a long time ago he had been involved with other women.

Omid didn't say anything and went to his room. When he woke up in the morning, he saw Sara had fallen asleep at the table. His heart went out to her. He quietly put on his shoes and sneaked out not to avoid waking her up. Omid liked her. He knew that none of the women he was dealing with would be like her, but he couldn't overcome his lust and compulsive desire for diversification.

At noon, Sarah's friends came to see her. One of them looked at Sarah and asked, "Why are your eyes puffy? Have you been crying?"

With a deep breath, having paused for a few seconds, Sarah replied, "My husband is out with his friends till late every night. He has relationships with other women. I have caught him red-handed several times. I'm fed up. I don't know what to do."

One of her friends sat beside her and embraced her. Another friend said, "If I were in your shoes, I would reciprocate; I would betray him. Such men should be punished in this way."

Sarah thought about it. She could easily betray him, but she didn't want to destroy her child's life because of her temptations.

The friend who was sitting beside her said, "You have to put out the fire; don't fan the flames. Sarah loves her life, and what you are suggesting isn't the right way." She looked at Sarah and said, "I will help you."

Sara asked, "How can you do?"

Her friend offered her a book and replied, "Read it! The sentences in this book will easily save you."

Sara seemed more bored and said, "Thank you; I have read a lot of books. I have even gone to the therapist. Everything will be fine for a short time, but then it will be worse than before."

Her friend said, "This book saved my life. My husband often went to his club with his friends. He often was backing home late at nights. I wanted to get divorced before I grabbed hold of this book. My husband and I saved our marital life and uttered the sentence in the book. After eight months, my husband was like the first days of our marriage and separated from his friends. He doesn't go to his club and now we have a peaceful life."

Sarah looked at her surprise and asked, "Really! How can it be? "

Her friend replied, "All the troubles you have, is a part of your destiny and perhaps will get worse in the future."

Sarah narrowed her eyes and asked, "What do you mean?"

Her friend replied, "All of us have had previous lives. We lived as rocks, plants, and animals and we died until we became human. We will die again to experience another life."

Sara asked, "What will this have to do with my destiny?"

Her friend replied, "By doing the good and evil actions in our past lives, we have acquired a perception which it has determined our destiny, how to live, in which family, with what name, in what place, with what religion and in what life quality."

Sarah asked with astonishment, "Do you want to say that our destiny is predetermined?"

Her friend replied, "Yes, as I said, we determined it with our deeds and behavior. Now in your life, you didn't have the opportunity to change your destiny's way by worshiping or benevolence or by reducing the negative effects, you must experience the way as it is."

Sara asked, "It means the same thing applies to my husband and this is his destiny?"

Her friend replied, "Yeah."

Another of Sarah's friend expressed, "That is not bad for him, he keeps enjoying his life?"

Sarah's friend who was sitting beside her said, "It seems doing these kinds of activities makes marriage grow cold, and it can ruin family life. He uses to do it, not to enjoy it and it's a part of his destiny. "

Sara asked, "What should I do?"

Her friend replied, "Changing the destiny has an easy solution, but not everybody can escape its power. I request you to read this book. Then you and your husband must repeat its sentences while thinking of your objective and intention."

Sara said, "Well, that's not difficult."

Her friend said, "It seems negative intelligence resides in your imagination and bodies, in order to survive they try to bring about conditions in which you refuse to utter the sentences."

Sara said, "What you are saying is like a matrix[1] movie."

---

[1] The American Australian sc*ience-fiction action film, directed and written by Vachovsky, was released in 1999. In this film, actors such as Keanu Reeves, Lawrence Fishburne, Kerry Ann Mass, Hugo Weaving, Joe Pantoliano, and Gloria Foster play. Matrix is a mix of action, martial arts and a multi-layer screenplay which screens a dystopia of the future community. In the movie, the humans perceive the reality in a forged world entitled "The Matrix" that was simulated by intelligent machinery to overcome the human population. While the heat and electrical activities of the human bodies were considered as a source of energy for machinery. Meanwhile, a computer programmer called Neo became aware of this fact and along with other people who left this dream world, rebelled against the machinery. The matrix movie is known for its heavy content and complex philosophical structure. The film is also a cyberpunk and sci-fi genre and includes numerous sources of philosophical and religious ideas.

There were moments of silence. Sarah took the book from her friend and thanked her for her kindness.

In the morning, Sarah was alone at home. She started reading the book with a passion, and then the painful senses were passed over her mind. She breathed deeply. She read a few pages of the book when she heard the doorbell. It was her son, Moses. She opened the door and kept on reading. It took a few minutes before the phone rang. She put the book on the table. It was one of her friends from college. It was a long time that she hadn't had heard from her. During their conversation, her friend told her about her good relationship with her husband, how much they loved each other and their romantic life. Sarah in her head began to compare and got frustrated and jealous. When her conversation was over, she said to herself, "Why should I go on with this life and dedicate myself to the child?" She looked at the book; reading the book made her angry and she refused to read on.

It took a few minutes. The emotional divorce in her life had hurt her, and she really from the bottom of heart wished her marital life would be resolved to save her life with all her power. With a deep breath, she remembered how she had helped their destitute neighbor the day before. God unconsciously appeared in the form of white light in her mind. The love force broke the intellectual knot in her mind and made her overcome the surroundings. She started concentrating. She didn't let anything distract her. Sarah went on reading the book and realized that by uttering the sentences only once everyone would abandon diversity and their lives would be on the right track. She said,

"Does it mean that Omid would give up the dissipation by saying these sentences once?

And that, by saying these sentences once, he would get rid of his vicious friends?

And that, tranquility and peace of mind would return to our home?"

It seemed very odd to her how the things would be put right by saying one sentence! She remembered her friend who had said by saying these sentences; her husband had been away from his vicious friends and had abandoned the longing for diversity. She thought, "By saying it, we will not lose anything; perhaps that's the way I've been looking for, for years."

Sarah looked at the introduction of the book which said, "By reading these sentences, the mind perceives the instinctive relationship with the Creator. The sentences help human mind to realize the power that exists to protect him from the negative intelligence devils and through one of the angels God's energy is used to change the mentality of negative intelligence that resides in the human subconscious and in the human body while leading our life, as well as it breaks down the sins committed during the previous lives that we have brought to our present life to define our destiny. Therefore, the frequencies of the mind are adjusted and people avoid friends who waste their time and who have weakened their personalities. As the personality strengthen and by cleansing the unconscious and souls off negative intelligence, one loses tendency toward diversity, leading to the destiny to fall on the right track."

Sarah read the sentences with the intention of reforming her life. Although she didn't understand anything, when she woke up the next day, she had spent a quiet night. She felt good. She had not been relaxed for years. She realized and was convinced that the sentences were effective and she was happy. She decided to ask Omid to utter the sentences once so that he would be relieved of the destiny that has caught him or might catch him. Only those who said the sentences with the intention of correcting their lives could easily pass the life's difficult tests.

At night when they were in bed and about to sleep, Sarah told Omid about what she had experienced the night before, and about the book, about what had made her relax the night before and what had caused her to become thought-free. She said, "Only by saying a simple and short sentence." Sarah looked into Omid's eyes; her gaze fascinated him and took the chance to think away from him. Initially, he was reluctant to say the sentence, but then since he also was fed up with his own lust for diversity and liked his life, he was convinced to read the sentences with the intention of improving his condition.

Now one year has passed since Sarah started to say the sentence. She is now relaxed and spends her days with peace of mind and tranquility. Sarah, thanks to her patience and tolerance, is delighted not only to have read the book but also to have succeeded in convincing Omid to say the sentence. After eight months, the vicious friends of Omid left him and now he has new friends who help him to improve his personality. Since Omid gave up the dissipation and forgot his youthful defeat, the conditions that were hurting them didn't happen anymore. His personality has grown and he spends his time with his family after work. Now Sarah has been able to promote the comfort and quality of her family by adjusting the eight-hour sleep plan, eating healthy home-cooked foods, encouraging family members to go to the club, planning short-term and long-term traveling with family members, encouraging family members to choose their favorite work.

The sentences which reading them once will help you give up the sexuality diversity,

Say in your heart that I read the sentence with the intention of reforming my life[1].

Now read the sentences quietly.

O light that all things are from you. Forgive the sins committed in my former and past lives. For the sake of forgiving my sins, I send the power of my love at all times to all the creatures in the world.

O light that whatever exists is yours; flow into my mind, so that the mentality of demons or any being who has shared my frequency to harm me, changes in the direction of existence, and those who are not reformed, breaks into their raw materials.

---

[1] *Make the intention and then read the sentences; remembering or repeating the sentences will shorten the duration of your improvement.*

O light that whatever exists is yours; open the channels for receiving my consciousness wider, so that I can realize the harm that I cause myself and my life.

In the Name of the Creator

Disturbing

Thoughts

Siamak pulled the last cigarette out of its pocket and lighted it. He had a firm puff. His eyes were full of tears. He was trembling. He couldn't expect even with one percent of the likelihood that such an incident would take place to be his antidote of these days. It was a grave defeat. He blamed himself, "Why didn't I do some query? Why didn't I give it a second thought before making a decision to choose her?"

Her wife had taken all his wealth as her dowry. Occasionally, he suffered a headache for having to think so much. He was drinking and smoking a lot to calm down. He was going through frustration and a very hard time. Negative thoughts rushed to his mind several times a day. The thoughts of the past didn't leave him. He was depressed. He was down and out.

Some time passed. He couldn't meet the ends to pay the installments of the loans which he had taken before. He got his transfer from the workplace and went to the capital city and started working there. After struggling he succeeded to rent a suite in the south of the town. He was no longer loyal to any religious framework. He found several girlfriends. At parties he was going, he got acquainted with a transsexual person and became friends with him. After having many conflicts with himself, he had been able to abandon his religious beliefs. He spent a few years in that little suite. He rented a larger house after he got rid of the settlement of his loans. Then, he changed his home appliances. He had progressed one step further.

Although years elapsed, the thought of his lost dowry, his failure in his love life, and hardship he had suffered were all disturbing him. He struggled to control his mind, but he was failed. It was difficult to accept the mistakes he had made.

He invited one of his college friends to his home. It was a long time since they had seen each other. After having lunch, as usual, Siamak lit a cigarette and had a puff, forgetting the fact that his friend didn't know anything about his smoking. He looked at Ehsan's eyes, which were watching him surprisingly.

Ehsan asked, "You didn't smoke. Did you?"

Siamak had a deep breath and replied, "When my wife and I got divorced, I gave her my whole wealth as her dowry. I could not even imagine that she had planned a plot against me. I have encountered many troubles during these years. Smoking makes me calm down."

Ehsan said, "Perhaps it makes you calm down for a few hours, but then you will feel worse."

Siamak looked at the cigarette smoke coming out of his mouth. Ehsan took a book out of his bag. There, on the pages of the book, some sentences were printed. He handed it to Siamak and commanded, "Say these sentences once in your mind."

Siamak had a look and asked, "What is it?"

Ehsan said, "I fell in love with a girl a year ago. She refused to marry me as I didn't have money. I was devastated. I was suffering from stress. My thought sensitivities increased. My brain worked in the opposite direction of my essence. I could not control my mind. I was close to being paralyzed. The past thoughts made me very nervous. Once I said these sentences, my mood became gradually fine, and the past thoughts that were disturbing me broke into pieces in my mind and disappeared. Go ahead and utter these sentences right away."

Siamak had a look at the sentences of the book and said, "Well, I said to them. What else should I do?"

Ehsan said, "Uttering the sentences once is enough. You will not need to control your mind anymore, the past thoughts that are bothering you will go away from your mind gradually and you will not compare yourself to anyone else. Comparing yourself to both others and your past personality is the fundamental cause of all troubles that haunt you through its consequences such as enmity, regret, jealousy, hatred and then grow."

Siamak said, "The thinking of the past takes/wastes my energy. If I can forget it, my energy will be much more. I can even compensate for my lost capital."

Ehsan said, "Good. But don't push yourself. Money is not worth as much as calmness. A man struggles to obtain money to reach peace of mind and tranquility aiming so that he can achieve her/his objectives. After a while, he realizes that the peace he was seeking was not there, and there was a mirage, indeed, he can find calmness just in himself. If he perceives the Creator, he will recognize his own strengths. Subsequently, he can identify the creatures that destroy his calmness. Then, he will attain peace of mind. It would be enough for the mind to figure out the relationships. That's what these sentences accomplish. By uttering them, actually, the mind will figure out the relationship that we have had since childhood and have protected us from the invasion of negative intelligence. It has weakened or has been partly disconnected due to weak religious knowledge, environmental pollution, and hiding of the negative intelligence. That's what the sacred books do. By reading them, the mind will notice the relationship caused that unwittingly negative intelligence goes away, gets destroyed or gets corrected. "

Siamak asked, "Do the sentences have an insinuation impact?"

Ehsan replied, "If it was insinuation, it would not have affected everyone by uttering them only once. But once saying the words one time, will permanently affect anybody with any ethnic, belief, cultural, national or religious origin."

Siamak said, "Everybody has some special thoughts that hurt him, some of which he keeps to himself and refuses to share them with others neither can he free his mind of them. They will waste his energy. If these sentences were available to everybody, they could benefit from them a lot."

Ehsan said, "These sentences won't be accessible by everyone. Lots of people don't have any awareness of them. Even if they were to be available to everyone, still most people would refuse to utter these simple sentences. They would laugh; they would ignore it or would skip the matter. Then, the virus of memories deceives them in order to reside in their minds. Some people must pass the life examinations through trial and error. They must strive to fight the difficult conditions of life. Such conditions were chosen by us before coming to this life to achieve the higher intelligence/perception and this is nature's choice. "

Siamak said, "I want to reach humanity in a peaceful manner. I don't want to experiment trial and error." Ehsan laughed and said, "So you want to make a shortcut. Both ways lead to the same destination, just the paths are different. One is short; the other one is hard and long."

Siamak asked, "How could it be possible to give up smoking?"

Ehsan suggested, "To quit smoking, use nylon and natural-friendly detergents." Siamak wondered, "What does this have to do with smoking?"

Ehsan explained, "When the component is alive, so the whole is alive. It means the earth is alive. We are observing the world within us. By harming the creatures around us, actually, we are harming ourselves. You are smoking because one day you have seriously damaged nature. Then, you have received poor protection and the negative intelligence has penetrated in you causing to hurt you too. Now that you have understood, stop doing it, and those sentences will certainly help you too."

One year after saying the sentences, Siamak forgot his past disturbing thoughts which wasted his energy. His mind was calm like a good as new. He is no longer worried about the future and stress, plus he doesn't think about the divorce. The past is not important to him, and he observes the world without any jealousy, regret, enmity, and hatred. He loves nature and its creatures. He gave up his smoking by repeating the sentences and by using the nature-friendly detergents and clean-energy vehicles.

The sentences which reading them once will help you forget the disturbing thoughts,

Say in your heart that I read the sentence with the intention of reforming my life[1].

Now read the sentences quietly.

O light that all things are from you. Forgive the sins committed in my former lives. For the sake of forgiving my sins, I send the power of my love at all times to all the creatures in the world. Help me to step in a way to compensate my sins.

O light that whatever exists is yours; flow into my mind, so that the mentality of demons or any being who has shared my frequency to harm me, changes in the direction of existence, and those who are not reformed, breaks into their raw materials.

[1] *Make the intention and then read the sentences; remembering or repeating the sentences will shorten the duration of your improvement.*

O light that whatever there is from you. Destroy the desires which were not materialized and became potential obstacles in the way, hindering my body from absorbing the energy of the universe. In this case, I can reconcile with life (the world) and will have a world (life) free of comparison.

In the Name of the Creator

Bribe

It was dark. The Ticking sound of the office clock was heard. All the employees but Milad had left. If he didn't work overtime, he wouldn't be able to take care of his loan payments. Milad looked at the files. There were still two more files that had to be recorded on the computer by him. He took a deep breath. Leaning back on his chair, he was gazing at the computer monitor. His colleague's suggestion had tempted him. He thought that if he regularly pays off his loan installments, it would take him ten years later.

As the filing task was completed, he went home. When he opened the entrance door, the smell of Ghormeh-Sabzi[1] had filled out the dining room. He inhaled deeply, saying, "Humm! What a good smell. Great!"

Coming towards Milad, Leila saluted him and said, "Welcome home, darling."

She took his briefcase and the bag of fruits from him before going to the kitchen. As soon as Ali saw him, he ran towards him and said, "Hurrah, dad..."

Milad hugged and kissed him. Sarah approached Milad and saluted her dad. Milad caressed her Sarah's head and kissed her forehead. Milad changed his clothes and returned to the dining room. He sat down at the dining table and told Leila,

---

[1] The delicious Iranian food.

"Thanks a lot. How did you know I have a craving for Ghormeh-Sabzi?"

Leila answered, "I am supposed to be your wife. You see how beautifully I have decorated the table."

Milad smiled and said, "Yes, my dear. Thank you."

Leila's look was full of love and affection. It could be possible to sense hope in her eyes. Milad got delighted to look at Leila's eyes. He forgot the feeling of tiredness of his working in the office when he faced his warm family relationship. On the other hand, he was upset that he could not spend more hours with them.

It was past midnight. Milad was lying on the bed. Contrary to the past nights, he could not sleep. His colleague's remarks were repeated in his mind, "How long will you be able to stay at the office till late at night and work overtime? Have you ever thought the hardship your family must go through, because of your stay so late at the office? They need you to be next to them to share your experiences with them. Consider the other employees; they have been placed in a good financial situation just in less than two years! Just put your hands in mines. In less than one year, you will make as much as ten years' salary you are earning now."

It was a moment of silence in his mind. His eyelids became heavier. Half asleep half awake, a sensation in his mind reminded him of the loss of love that he had experienced during his youth. The disturbing thoughts of the past were coming back to his mind and made him nervous (stimulating subconscious cells for a relationship and accepting information) then, he was engaged in his religious beliefs. His colleague's suggestion passed through the self-consciousness filter and entered the subconscious. In the depths of the subconscious, it carved on the cells that were ready to accept this information, and then he fell asleep. The next morning, Milad went to his colleague's room to give the positive response. It was decided for him to cooperate with several of his colleagues in forwarding the requests of some customers and reduce their taxes by the bribe.

Years passed. The kids grew older. Ali was adolescent and Sarah went to college. Milad had a good financial situation and had settled all his loans. He had a villa with all the facilities in a good district of the city, a high-model car, and a good amount of money saved in his bank. It was time for dinner. The restaurant courier delivered the ordered foods. Ali opened the door of his room. He came towards the foods and took one of them frowning. Milad was sitting down on the sofa and he was watching the TV. He glanced at Ali and asked, "Why didn't you say hi?"

Ali smirked and quietly said, "Get out here..."

Milad had a remarkable look at Ali. He hardly controlled himself so that he would not be involved with him. Ali was arrogant and stubborn. He had a lot of verbal conflicts with him. Milad put his food on the table and started eating it. When eating of his food was over, Leila while applying the cucumber mask on her face, just came out of her room. He threw his voice in his throat and asked, "So where is this girl during recent two or three days?"

Leila replied, "She called. She says that I'm on a trip with my friends and I don't return until the end of the week."

Milad got angry and tightly put the glass of the water on the table and said, "She had no right to travel without any permission. It seems she doesn't have any parents. Do you know who her friends are? Whose persons does she communicate with?"

Leila said, "I cannot stand for her."

Milad complained, "The girl whose mother is you will not get better than this. You are busy twenty-four hours with your appearance."

The quarrel started as usual and rose. Leila went to her room and slammed the door behind her. Because of going back and forth to his room, Milad's grandmother had found out about the disagreements and coldness among Milad's family members. She was worried about the consequences. She reported the matter to Milad's grandfather. After a week, the grandfather held a party and invited all the children, grandchildren, daughters-in-law, and one of his old friends who was an experienced and educated man, to make a speech about moving in the right direction in the life and the consequences of deviation from the righteousness. Before starting the celebration, grandfather's friend began to speak, saying, "One of the greatest efforts of living beings is having a strong and healthy generation. However, it is not possible for all of the living creatures. Lots of generations involved in the pest in the beginning or when they grow up to some extent. They don't grow up well or get extinct. If we have the basis, simple, and powerful information, we can breed the generations that are away from lots of pests. This, in turn, can help to have a healthy community and generation. In general, my talks commence from the beginning of our creation. It will terminate after explaining the path of creation and the end of this way. Also, I will explain how we can make this path smoother or change our predetermined destiny. "

The grandfather's friend went on, "Look. Notice that every flow that originates from a source returns to the same source. The produced flow is part of its source and reflects the reactions and relationships of the components within that source. Our creation begins with the imagination of a great being and continues until we become God and dominate the world inside ourselves and rejoin the Creator. There is a lot of life and death between the beginning and the end of this cycle. There is the world of rocks, plants, animals, humans, ghosts, hyper ghost, super ghost, and the other stages until we become God and dominate the world inside ourselves. Notice that when we talk about the world of rocks we mean life and death in all kinds of rocks. When we say the world of plants we mean life in all the species of plants."

One of the grandchildren asked, "Does this life and death cycle also exist among humans?"

The grandfather's friend replied, "Yes, there is a cycle between the color of the skin or the religions."

The grandfather's friend paused and continued, "Something that accompanies us throughout the phases from the beginning to elevating to divinity is a kind of essence known as the essence of existence, in which all experiences of emotions and positive or negative actions throughout all stages of our lives are recorded. By passing each stage, a pearl of wisdom resulting from the good and bad deeds in the previous stages is achieved. This issue determines our destiny in the current life that we are in which family, nationality, with what name and being in what level of intelligence and thought?"

One of the daughters-in-law asked, "Wisdom for what thing?"

The grandfather's friend replied, "For understanding creation and the universe."

The daughter-in-law asked, "Are the animals aware of being?"

The grandfather's friend replied, "Yes, even the particles of stones and plants are intelligent and there is the good and bad behavior among them."

One of the grandfather's children wondered with a smile, "Do they have the heaven and the hell?"

The grandfather's friend explained, "The heaven and hell are at the interval of the social classes, which are at every stage from the stage of being stone to the being of God. By passing each stage, the convenience of heaven and hell will increase. The creatures who are well-positioned, having good conditions and in general, having welfare are placed in heaven, and those who are in distress and in difficult conditions are in the hell. No creature is in the absolute hell or in the absolute heaven. Since no creature in its entire life could be absolutely evil or no creature could be also absolutely fine, so every creature belonging to every class has deficiency and defect."

The eldest grandfather's child asked, "It means we don't have the authority and everything is predetermined?"

The grandfather's friend replied, "By attaining the wisdom resulting from the good and evil deeds, which is recorded on the essence of existence, everything is predetermined unconsciously, like our shape and appearance. According to our right evaluation of the amount of absorbing energy from the angels of death, wealth, consciousness, in order to specify the laws or moving path, also our family condition and the other circumstances which are not chosen by us, our destiny would be determined. "

The eldest grandfather's child said with a smile, "Let's eat and sleep, and not try?"

The grandfather's friend expressed, "Everyone attempts as much energy as he can absorb from the angel of laws or movement. If we consider the communication path with this angel is as the channels around our chakra, a part of the channel communicates with the angel and in another section of it, the negative intelligence is living. This negative intelligence prevents us from stopping and merely eating and sleeping. Unconsciously, we reject what we have been saying, or we get tired very soon and try again.

The amount of this effort has been set for every living being throughout its entire life, and the increase it requires the correction of the negative intelligence present in the channels. If we deliberately try to shuffle these rules inside ourselves, it will take lots of our energy and there is no benefit only harm."

The grandfather requested, "Can you explain more?"

The grandfather's friend explained, "Not everyone gets wealthy and achieving wealth does not relate/depend on the great effort. If this were the case, then the laborers who struggle and work more than anybody else would get more wealth. Getting wealth depends on the amount of intensity association with its angel. It's the same for the lifetime, too. Those who eat good and healthy foods are those who have a stronger relationship with the angel of life. Not everyone eats good and healthy food, even though they are aware of the benefits of healthy food."

The grandmother asked, "It means that even if we want to, we won't be able to eat healthy foods?"

The grandfather's friend replied, "You will get tired very soon and return to the initial state. Because the presence of the negative intelligence in poor parts of the channels that are associated with the angel of life doesn't let/prevents you have/having a steady and long-term moving in that direction and you will unconsciously return to the initial state. The association with the angel of consciousness is also the same."

The grandmother continued asking, "What is the role of Satan?"

The grandfather's friend replied, "If we assume our world to be a large aquarium, this creature will be like a mud eater/catfish who feeds with our negative feelings like jealousy, hatred, enmity, greed, and other negative qualities. The devils, which are of the kind of every being in its own sort and also invisible negative intelligence are living on Earth, unknowingly help feed the Satan and the Satan lives in the sky."

One of the grandchildren said, "Those people who are thieves and murderers and felons are not guilty?"

The grandpa's friend explained, "There are good and bad attributes in every personality, even in the theft. In history, there were numbers of thieves who stole from the people who were rich and robbed the poor fellows of money and then distributed among the poor men. However, they took a portion of it for themselves. They were fair robbers. All of the various personalities in a community have been planned by God in order to have a movement, and everyone contributes as much to his wisdom. Usually, every human being who doesn't have enough intelligence gets bad roles, and this is the hell and burning in the fire inside. Because he needs to try more for his true personality, humanity."

The eldest grandfather's child said, "So we don't have any authority?"

The grandfather's friend said, "We have only the authority of doing good and bad deeds at every stage of our life that will elevate the quality of the path. But the essential destiny doesn't change."

The eldest grandfather's child continued, "There is no way to change our destiny?"

The grandpa's friend said, "Unless we use the power of love to love ourselves and all living beings, and the easiest way to accomplish this is to do great or excessive charitable actions."

The grandfather asked, "Can you give us an example of how this happens?"

The grandpa's friend expressed, "As I mentioned, all living beings have the connections with angels of consciousness, death, laws or movement and wealth. When we are good to them, they will pray for us so unconsciously their minds will be set in a state that will connect us to the angel with whom they have a stronger relationship. The intensity and the quality of this connection will cause the negative intelligence present in our weak channels either to change their mentality, or going far away, or be vanished, or extended the entrance entry to receive the energies of some angels into the chakras. Therefore, if the creature that has been affected by our good action is associated with the angel of wealth, our financial situation will get better. If there is a stronger connection with the angel of consciousness, then our understanding and perception will become greater, and if it has a stronger relationship with the angel of death, we will find a long longevity, and if it is accompanied by the angel of motion or laws, our attempts will be increased to reach our goals and our destiny will be changed."

The grandpa asked, "What kind of good and bad deeds has the greatest impact on changing our fate?"

The grandpa's friend explained, "The greatest good action that has a great effect on opening the channels of connection to the angels is to favor the parents and especially the mother. Because she has the greatest and the strongest connections with the children's minds. One of the worst guiltiest is abusing people and violating the legal rights of the people which endanger the life, property, and honor of them. That is rising in today's societies. Those who commit these sins weaken the entrance entry to receive the energy of their consciousness channels. So the negative intelligence gains more power and infects the consciousness that comes from the universe. In this condition, the power of love is weakened inside the person. Against, the negative senses, such as hatred, pride, jealousy, regret and etc. gain more power. Positive connections between the family members are disrupted, and life becomes cold and spiritless. The family-unfriendly behaviors can lead family members more to use drugs, commit suicide, murder, and so on." Milad dried up when he heard the talks of the grandfather's friend. His head started to ache. He touched his forehead with his hand and pressed it. Now he can understand why his life doesn't have the former warmth and love. He was alarmed out for his children.

The grandfather's friend drank a little tea and said, "At the end, the life of a person who brings the Halal(permitted) money to his life will be ahead of one who earns the Haram(prohibited) money and eventually has more wealth, just like the story of the competition between the rabbit and the turtle. The one who earns the forbidden property has a big house, a high-model car, more capital, also has an addicted child. Against, the one who gains the Halal money has a small house, doesn't own any cars, but has a healthy, well-educated and great-honored child who enjoys just by looking at her/him. Finally, the one who has stepped in the right direction will be more successful, because he can enjoy his life more after many years of hard work."

The grandmother gestured to her husband with a twinkle to ask his friend a question with such an implication, so that Milad could indirectly realize his wrong way.

The grandfather asked, "If a person took bribe money or obtains property in a wrong way, what should he do?"

The grandfather's friend took out several books from his bag and handed his audience and said that if someone took a bribe money and feels that he has earned his money in a wrong way, he has to make an intention and sign inside the relevant boxes of the book so he can give up taking the bribe. It would be better for all of his family members who have used this forbidden money to make an intention do sign then, their bodies would be cleaned of negative intelligence and the destiny will be put in its true path toward humanity. "

The grandmother asked, "How is this happening?"

The grandpa's friend said, "By doing this, you will connect to the angel and the negative intelligence will find a positive mentality or they will vanish then, you will not be bribed anymore. The next work that you have to do is consult with a diligent spiritual advisor so you can do money laundering which has been earned through this way relative to your debt. It takes seven years to change all the cells in your body and make new ones with laundered money again. After you sign and purge your money from the Haram property, love and affection will gradually return to your life. "

By ending the speech of the grandfather's friend, the daughters-in-law brought the fruits and started the celebration.

Milad read the book. After making the intention, he signed inside the frames. Six months later, taking the bribe was abandoned. His family members also signed inside the frame of their books. He, with the help of Leila, seriously cleared his property off the bribes he had taken and the money which really didn't belong to him. During the seven years, the love and affection gradually returned to their home and Milad's family lived peacefully ever after.

Once you sign inside the following boxes, you will leave to take the bribe forever and your bodies will be erased from the destructive effects of the negative intelligence.

Make an intention and complete the following boxes.[1]

With the intention of forgiving the sins of your previous and past lives, sign inside the following box[2].

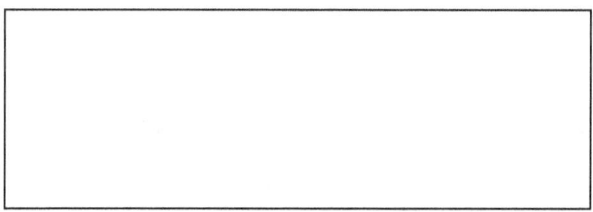

With the intention of changing the mentality of the devils or any other entity that is aligned with your mind, sign inside the following box in the right direction.

es; remembering

duration of your

---

[2] *Just sign inside the box.*

With the intention of not comparing yourself with others sign inside the following box.